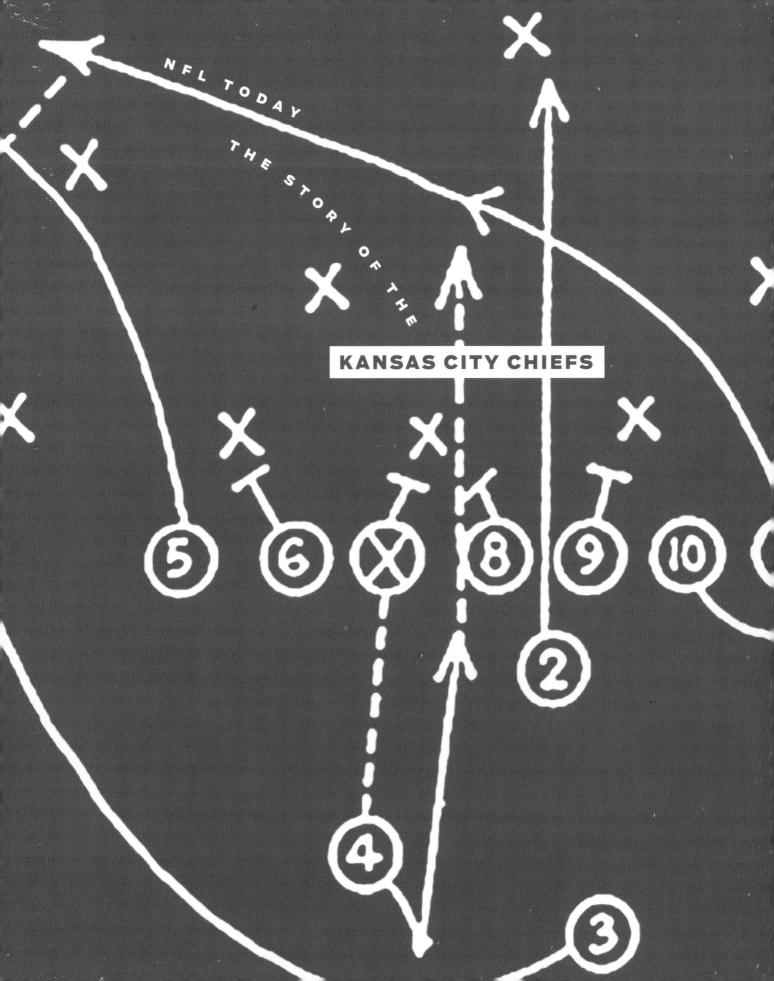

NFL TODAY

THE STORY OF THE KANSAS CITY CHIEFS

NATE FRISCH

CREATIVE EDUCATION

PUBLISHED BY CREATIVE EDUCATION
P.O. BOX 227, MANKATO, MINNESOTA 56002
CREATIVE EDUCATION IS AN IMPRINT OF THE CREATIVE COMPANY
WWW.THECREATIVECOMPANY.US

DESIGN AND PRODUCTION BY BLUE DESIGN
ART DIRECTION BY RITA MARSHALL
PRINTED IN THE UNITED STATES OF AMERICA

PHOTOGRAPHS BY GETTY IMAGES (BRIAN BAHR,
VERNON BIEVER/NFL, JAY BIGGERSTAFF/TUSP,
RICH CLARKSON/SPORTS ILLUSTRATED, JONATHAN
DANIEL/STRINGER, STEPHEN DUNN, JAMES FLORES/
NFL, FOCUS ON SPORT, GEORGE GOJKOVICH, ROD
HANNA/NFL, TOM HAUCK, JEFF HAYNES/AFP, ANDY
HAYT, WESLEY HITT, WALTER IOOSS JR./SPORTS
ILLUSTRATED, PAUL JASIENSKI, DAVE KAUP/AFP,
DAVID E. KLUTHO/SPORTS ILLUSTRATED, G. NEWMAN
LOWRANCE, NFL PHOTOS, DARRYL NORENBERG/NFL,
PANORAMIC IMAGES, JOE ROBBINS, JAMIE SQUIRE,
RICK STEWART, DAMIAN STROHMEYER/SPORTS
ILLUSTRATED, AL TIELEMANS/SPORTS ILLUSTRATED,
TIM UMPHREY, RON VESELY)

COPYRIGHT © 2014 CREATIVE EDUCATION

LIBRARY OF CONGRESS CATALOGING-IN-PUBLICATION DATA
FRISCH, NATE.
THE STORY OF THE KANSAS CITY CHIEFS / BY NATE FRISCH.
P. CM. — (NFL TODAY)
INCLUDES INDEX.
SUMMARY: THE HISTORY OF THE NATIONAL FOOTBALL LEAGUE'S
KANSAS CITY CHIEFS, SURVEYING THE FRANCHISE'S BIGGEST
STARS AND MOST MEMORABLE MOMENTS FROM ITS INAUGURAL
SEASON IN 1960 TO TODAY.
ISBN 978-1-60818-307-4
1. KANSAS CITY CHIEFS (FOOTBALL TEAM)—HISTORY—JUVENILE
LITERATURE. I. TITLE.

GV956.K35F77 2013
796.332'6409778411—DC23   2012031216

FIRST EDITION
9 8 7 6 5 4 3 2 1

COVER: RUNNING BACK JAMAAL CHARLES
PAGE 2: CORNERBACK BRANDON FLOWERS
PAGES 4–5: LINEBACKER SHERRILL HEADRICK
PAGE 6: QUARTERBACK LEN DAWSON

TABLE OF CONTENTS

DOWNTOWN KANSAS CITY IS KNOWN FOR ITS ARTS, SHOPPING, AND DINING

From Cowboys to Indians

t the beginning of the 19th century, the land where Kansas City, Missouri, now sits represented a sort of boundary between the civilized and untamed halves of America. In 1827, Independence, Missouri, was established and became a starting point for settlers making long trips west along what became known as the Oregon, California, and Santa Fe trails. A decade later, when Kansas City started growing about 10 miles from Independence, it too served as a gateway to the west. Today, the midwestern city is headquarters to many major businesses and is noted for its contributions to jazz and blues music, not to mention its unique style of barbecue.

In 1963, "K.C." also became home to a professional football team called the Chiefs. The club, though, had its roots in Texas. Since the 1920s, the National Football League (NFL) had been the dominant brand of professional football in America, and Texas

EARLY GREAT WILLIE LANIER WAS ONE OF FOOTBALL'S FIRST BLACK STAR LINEBACKERS

Lamar Hunt

TEAM FOUNDER, OWNER / TEXANS/CHIEFS SEASONS: 1959–2006

Lamar Hunt earned the nickname "Games" for being a huge sports fan when he was a reserve tight end on the Southern Methodist University football team. After founding the Texans (who became the Chiefs) and spearheading the AFL, Hunt extended his reach far beyond football with the creation of a tennis league (World Championship Tennis) and team ownership in basketball (the National Basketball Association's Chicago Bulls) and minor league baseball (the Dallas–Fort Worth Spurs). But among his biggest achievements was jump-starting the "other football" in America with the North American Soccer League (NASL) in 1967. He owned the Dallas Tornado franchise, which went on to win the NASL championship in 1971. After the NASL discontinued its operations, Hunt kept his ownership hand in soccer through three Major League Soccer teams: the Kansas City Wizards, Columbus Crew, and FC Dallas. A member of many different sports halls of fame, Hunt was the first AFL member inducted into the Pro Football Hall of Fame in 1972. "He loved sports so much," his wife Norma said. "He was so passionate about them, and he wanted others to share the joy."

HANK STRAM (LEFT) PROVED TO BE A BRILLIANT HIRE AS THE TEXANS' FIRST COACH

millionaire Lamar Hunt wanted to move an existing NFL team to the city of Dallas or create an expansion team there. The NFL declined his request. Since Hunt couldn't be a part of the existing league, he decided to create his own. He found wealthy peers who also wanted to own football teams, and together they formed the American Football League (AFL).

Hoping to appeal to the entire potential fan base in the huge state of Texas, Hunt named his team the Texans. To further enhance regional interest, he filled much of his roster with players who had competed at Texas colleges. Among those players was swift and sizable running back Abner Haynes. In the AFL's inaugural 1960 season, Haynes led the league in rushing yards and caught 55 passes on his way to earning the Rookie of the Year and Player of the Year awards.

Guiding the development of Haynes and the rest of the Texans' roster was head coach Hank Stram, who'd previously been an assistant coach at the University of Miami. Stram's combination of ingenuity, interpersonal skills, and enthusiasm allowed him to revolutionize how football was played and to coax maximum effort from his players. He would go on to lead the team for 15 years.

 unt had seemingly made excellent personnel and business decisions. However, after he established the AFL and his Dallas-based team, the NFL quickly countered by creating the Dallas Cowboys in 1960 in an effort to squash interest in the competing new league. And as the Texans went a middling 14–14 over the course of their first two seasons, they had trouble drawing fans.

In 1962, the Texans added little-used NFL quarterback Len Dawson, a player Stram had previously coached at Purdue University. After floundering between the Pittsburgh Steelers and the Cleveland Browns, Dawson's confidence had waned, and his skills had eroded. But Stram believed Dawson was still a great quarterback who just needed a fresh start.

Stram's gamble was a triumph. In 1962, Dawson led the surprising Texans to the AFL Western Division title and the AFL Championship Game. Dawson emerged as a star as he led the AFL in completion percentage and tossed a league-high 29 touchdowns. "There is no passer in professional football more accurate than Lenny," Stram said.

Dawson didn't do it all by himself, though. Haynes scored a league-record 19 touchdowns to go along with 1,622 total yards, while linebacker Sherrill Headrick and cornerback Dave Grayson spearheaded a fierce defense. In the 1962 AFL Championship Game, these players carried the Texans to a 20–17

Bouncy Bowl

Unhappy with the wordy title "AFL-NFL World Championship Game," Lamar Hunt coined the name "Super Bowl" by accident in 1966. Hunt recalled that during owner meetings about playoff game structuring, he tried to reference the final game, and out slipped the term "Super Bowl." Many other team owners in both leagues thought the name was too funny, but most agreed it was snappy. They tried to come up with a better name, but no one could, and so it stuck. "My own feeling is that it probably registered in my head because my daughter, Sharron, and my son, Lamar Jr., had a children's toy called a Super Ball," Hunt explained, "and I probably interchanged the phonetics of 'bowl' and 'ball.'" After two years, Hunt's "Super Bowl" became the name of the game. That year, in a note to NFL commissioner Pete Rozelle, Hunt suggested adding roman numerals to give the game "more dignity." So, after the third Super Bowl, roman numerals were grandfathered in and added to the first trio of games. And the Super Bowl as we know it was named forever.

THE CHIEFS EARNED RENOWN FOR TAKING PART IN THE VERY FIRST SUPER BOWL

WITH LEN DAWSON HEADING THE OFFENSE, THE CHIEFS MADE FOUR PLAYOFF RUNS

overtime victory over their intrastate rivals, the Houston Oilers.

Despite the Texans' championship, Hunt had decided that Dallas wasn't big enough for two teams, and he relocated his club to Kansas City before the start of the 1963 season. General manager Jack Steadman convinced Hunt that the proud American Indian moniker "Chiefs" was better suited to represent the Missouri city, and the Kansas City Chiefs were born. Although the great play of Dawson and Haynes quickly won over new fans in the "Show Me State," the Chiefs were a mediocre team in their first two seasons there, going 5–7–2 and 7–7.

Len Dawson

QUARTERBACK / TEXANS/CHIEFS SEASONS: 1962–75 / HEIGHT: 6 FEET / WEIGHT: 190 POUNDS

Len Dawson was exactly what coach Hank Stram needed to complete his championship-team assembly. Perhaps more importantly, Stram believed Dawson could lead the Chiefs for the long haul. Although Dawson was the top draft pick taken by the Pittsburgh Steelers in 1957, he floundered there and was traded to the Cleveland Browns. But Stram signed him in 1962 and let him fly. After starting only 2 games and throwing just 45 passes in his first 5 NFL seasons, Dawson had a positive and immediate effect on the Texans/Chiefs. He led the team to an AFL championship in his first season and earned the nickname "Lenny the Cool" with his calm, composed in-game demeanor and reserved personality off the field. "He was the quiet assassin," running back Ed Podolak said. "He could say more with a stare than most players could with words. He was the team leader, no doubt about it." While Dawson compiled impressive passing statistics, it never was about the numbers for this field general, because he focused completely on winning. "Lenny was our man," receiver Otis Taylor said. "He was our leader."

SIDELINE STORIES

Stram on Record

Today, the NFL Films studio commonly uses portable microphones to put television viewers within earshot of the on-field action. Many coaches, players, and officials have been asked to wear microphones over the years. But the first such request went to Hank Stram, one of football's most colorful characters, in Super Bowl IV after the 1969 season. And in the process, NFL Films captured an in-depth look at a good-natured coach winning the game of his life. Viewers got to watch and hear Stram as he energetically coached and quipped all game long. He posed one of the most common coach-to-official questions in the history of sports: "How in the world can all six of you miss a play like that?" But perhaps the most fascinating moment was his prediction that the play "Sixty-five Toss Power Trap" to running back Mike Garrett would break for a touchdown. The recorded spotlight served Stram well after his coaching tenure ended. He spent 18 years calling *Monday Night Football* games on the radio alongside legendary broadcaster Jack Buck. His trademark was his ability to accurately predict the next play.

HANK STRAM SHARED HIS SUPER BOWL IV INSIGHTS LIVE WITH THE ENTIRE WORLD

Highest Highs, Lowest Lows

In 1965, the Chiefs bolstered their offense by drafting Otis Taylor, a receiver with the complete package of size, speed, strength, and agility. Taylor also had confidence. "I'll tell you something about Otis Taylor," he said of himself. "He wants to be the best—always. There hasn't been a year when he didn't want to score more touchdowns than anybody and gain more yardage than anybody. At the start of the season, I aim for the top 10 and higher. And I don't quit."

In 1966, powerful linebackers Bobby Bell and E. J. Holub helped the Chiefs win the Western Division and pound the Buffalo Bills 31–7 in the AFL Championship Game to bring home the franchise's second league title. In previous seasons, that would have been the ultimate accomplishment. But the AFL had established itself as a major sports attraction, and its champion was set to take on the NFL's champion in the first Super Bowl

DEFENSIVE END JERRY MAYS (#75) AND LINEBACKER BOBBY BELL (#78)

✕ Hank Stram

During the decade-long history of the AFL, Hank Stram won more games and more league championships (1962, 1966, 1969) than any other coach and was the only coach in the AFL's history to take his team to two Super Bowls, winning one. Stram was known for his creative innovations. On offense, he developed the "moving pocket," which took advantage of quarterback Len Dawson's scrambling ability. He also devised the "two-tight-end" alignment, which provided an extra blocker and helped slow down the opposition's pass rush. On defense, he created the "stack defense." This positioned the linebackers behind the defensive linemen, allowing the linebackers to react more quickly to the opposing offense. He also always used a nose tackle across from center. These innovations helped Stram mine the most out of his players' talents. Willie Lanier, Bobby Bell, and Jim Lynch were considered by many to be the best linebacker trio in the AFL. By 2013, Stram and six of his Chiefs players—Dawson, Lanier, Bell, Buck Buchanan, Emmitt Thomas, and Jan Stenerud—were enshrined in the Pro Football Hall of Fame.

"He was the quiet assassin."

**ED PODOLAK ON
LEN DAWSON**

to determine a true world champion. The Chiefs faced the Green Bay Packers and their legendary coach, Vince Lombardi, in Super Bowl I.

The heavily favored Packers scored first. Although the Chiefs struggled offensively, Dawson tied the game in the second quarter with a touchdown pass to dependable fullback Curtis McClinton. But the Packers and their talented quarterback, Bart Starr, proved too powerful for the young Chiefs and pulled away in the second half to win 35–10.

After going 9–5 in 1967, Kansas City improved to 12–2 in 1968 and tied for first in the Western Division with their archrivals, the Oakland Raiders, who soundly beat the Chiefs 41–6 in the playoffs. Undaunted by the ouster, Kansas City came back stronger than ever in 1969 behind a hard-hitting defense that featured star linebacker Willie Lanier and bruising tackle Junious "Buck" Buchanan. After narrowly beating the New York Jets 13–6 in the playoffs, the Chiefs dispatched Oakland 17–7 in the championship game—the final game in AFL history. With tremendous momentum, they made a triumphant return to the Super Bowl, where they met the Minnesota Vikings.

Most football fans expected the Vikings to win Super Bowl IV. But kicker Jan Stenerud booted three field goals to give Kansas City an early 9–0 lead. After the Chiefs recovered a fumbled Vikings kickoff, running back Mike Garrett plunged in for a touchdown. With the score 16–7 in the third quarter, Dawson hit Taylor with a short pass and watched the star receiver high-step for a 46-yard touchdown, sealing a

A Paige in the History Books

During his nine-season stay in Kansas City, receiver Stephone Paige (pictured above, right) was considered a third-down player, but he never lost confidence in his abilities. "If I can make plays on third down," Paige wondered, "why can't I make them on first down? It's time to turn me loose." In the 1985 season finale against the San Diego Chargers, Paige was turned loose. And in the process, he broke Cleveland Rams receiver Jim Benton's 40-year-old NFL single-game receiving record of 303 yards. The plucky Paige went over 100 yards in the first quarter on just 2 catches. He had amassed 258 yards by the second quarter, which broke the Chiefs' single-game receiving record—in the first half! Paige hurt his ribs in the second quarter but returned late in the third to grab a 39-yard pass. Then, with about 5 minutes left in the game, Paige caught a 12-yarder that broke the record by 6 yards—309 total. Chiefs quarterback Bill Kenney admitted later he was determined to help Paige hit the mark "if I had to throw the ball to him five straight times."

OTIS TAYLOR LED ALL NFL WIDEOUTS WITH 1,110 RECEIVING YARDS IN 1971

23–7 Chiefs victory. "Our game plan wasn't very complicated," said Dawson, who was named Super Bowl Most Valuable Player (MVP). "It involved throwing a lot of formations at them—formations they hadn't seen during the course of the season."

In 1970, when the AFL merged with the NFL, the Chiefs slipped to 7–5–2. But in 1971, they met the Miami Dolphins in an epic, double-overtime playoff game. The usually reliable Stenerud missed a field goal as regulation time expired, then missed another game-winning opportunity in overtime. Finally, the Dolphins' Garo Yepremian kicked a field goal in the second overtime to hand the Chiefs a heartbreaking 27–24 loss. The 82-minute and 40-second marathon still stands as the longest contest in NFL history.

Despite some great performances by scrappy halfback Ed Podolak, Coach Stram's squad then slid out of contention. A move into the new Arrowhead Stadium in 1972 provided some excitement, but the team continued to struggle. Still, faithful Chiefs fans showed up to cheer for such Pro-Bowlers as cornerback Emmitt Thomas and nose tackle Curley Culp.

Hank Stram was fired after the 1974 season, Dawson and Taylor both retired in 1975, and the Chiefs slipped into the bottom half of the American Football Conference (AFC) West Division. Even as new heroes emerged, including hard-hitting defensive end Art Still, losing became a habit in Kansas City. Paul

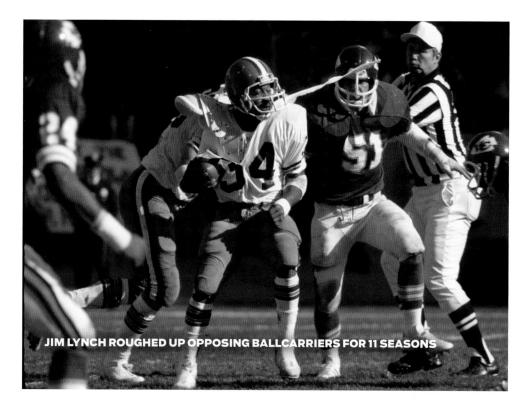
JIM LYNCH ROUGHED UP OPPOSING BALLCARRIERS FOR 11 SEASONS

Wiggin, Stram's successor, oversaw back-to-back 5–9 seasons. Then, in 1977, after the team started 1–6, Hunt fired Wiggin in midseason, and the Chiefs finished with a franchise-worst 2–12 record.

nder new coach Marv Levy, the Chiefs climbed to a respectable 8–8 in 1980. The team's future looked bright when it drafted running back Joe Delaney in 1981. At 5-foot-10 and 184 pounds, Delaney was small in stature. But he made up for it with quick feet and a big heart, and he galloped 1,121 yards to earn AFC Rookie of the Year honors. With a stout defense led by ballhawking safety Gary Barbaro, the Chiefs improved to 9–7.

Then, after a strike-shortened 1982 season, tragedy struck on June 29, 1983. That afternoon, in an act of heroism, Delaney died while trying to save three boys from drowning near his home in Monroe, Louisiana. His teammates took the young star's passing hard. "Everyone knew he was a great football player," guard Tom Condon said. "But that was only a small part of what made him so special to us. As a young rookie, he played with cracked ribs, a broken wrist, a sprained knee.... When those little kids needed help, he gave up his life trying to save them. He wasn't a swimmer.... The man had a tremendous heart—he was special."

The Battle to Brag

The Governor's Cup trophy has been a staple of Missouri pro football for more than 40 years. The preseason—and sometimes regular-season—contest between the Chiefs and their intrastate rivals, the St. Louis Rams, has been referred to as "The Battle of Missouri" or "I-70 Series." The tradition started in 1968 against the St. Louis Cardinals. When the Cardinals moved to Arizona in 1987, the Chiefs held a dominant 16–7–2 advantage in the rivalry. The series resumed in 1995 when the Los Angeles Rams relocated to St. Louis. It took on new meaning in 2001 when the Chiefs hired former Rams coach Dick Vermeil. After molding the Rams into one of the most powerful offensive squads in NFL history and winning Super Bowl XXXIV, Vermeil installed the same offense in Kansas City. In the early 2000s, the teams boasted two of the most productive offenses in the NFL, and what used to be a sometimes-meaningless game became a high-energy shootout for state bragging rights. While the Chiefs were 5–9 in the preseason against the Rams (by 2013), they were 5–0 in the all-important regular season.

THE CITIES OF KANSAS CITY AND ST. LOUIS ARE ONLY ABOUT 250 MILES APART

MARTY SCHOTTENHEIMER COACHED IN KANSAS CITY FOR A DECADE

The Schottenheimer Era

After Delaney's death, the 1983 Chiefs slipped to 6–10. Levy had been fired, and new coach John Mackovic took over. By 1986, Mackovic rebuilt the team into a surprise contender, largely through special-teams play. With 11 blocked kicks and 6 return touchdowns (off blocks and punt and kickoff returns), special teams helped the Chiefs make the postseason for the first time in 15 years. But it was in and out, as they lost to the Jets 35–15.

Frustrated, Hunt shook up the franchise in December 1988. His first move was to hire general manager Carl Peterson, who had previously guided the Philadelphia Eagles, and give him complete control over the team's operations. Peterson moved quickly to name former Cleveland Browns head coach Marty Schottenheimer as the team's new sideline leader. "I believe the opportunity is there with this football team to once again approach that great tradition of the Kansas City Chiefs," said Schottenheimer. "My principal

A HARD-CHARGING CHRISTIAN OKOYE WAS AN INTIMIDATING SIGHT IN THE '80s

Jan Stenerud

KICKER / CHIEFS SEASONS: 1967–79 / HEIGHT: 6-FOOT-2 / WEIGHT: 187 POUNDS

Who would ever have thought that a college basketball coach and a skier would alter the course of football kicking forever? Jan Stenerud attended Montana State University in the early 1960s on a skiing scholarship. During his sophomore year, he was spotted by the college's basketball coach as he was booming footballs "soccer style," or from the side. Football coach Jim Sweeney was contacted immediately. "[Sweeney] saw me a couple of weeks later running the stadium steps," Stenerud recalls, "and he hollered at me, 'Hey, get down here. I hear you can kick.' So I kicked a few in front of the team. And they thought I had a chance, and they decided I should go out for spring practice." Stenerud starred for the next two years, during which he once kicked a then collegiate-record 59-yard field goal. Stenerud wasn't pro football's first soccer-style kicker, but he was arguably the best. He also never missed a game. At the time of his retirement, he ranked behind only George Blanda in all-time NFL scoring and later became the first pure placekicker elected to the Pro Football Hall of Fame.

NEIL SMITH WAS A PASS-RUSHING SENSATION THROUGHOUT THE EARLY 1990s

reason for selecting this opportunity is that I believe we can win—and win very, very quickly."

Schottenheimer installed "Marty Ball," an offense that featured Christian Okoye, a gigantic (6-foot-2 and 260 pounds) running back nicknamed "The Nigerian Nightmare." Okoye would lead the team in rushing for 3 seasons, including a club-record 1,480-yard effort in 1989. That year also saw the development of young defensive talent, including outstanding end Neil Smith and aggressive linebacker Derrick Thomas. This ferocious duo anchored a defense that emerged as one of the NFL's best.

Kansas City earned its first playoff victory in 22 years by beating the Los Angeles Raiders 10–6 in the 1991 playoffs. Running back Barry Word pummeled the Raiders with a Chiefs postseason-record 130 rushing yards, and the defense stripped away 6 turnovers. Although the Chiefs lost to the Buffalo Bills in the next round, Schottenheimer had his team believing that greatness was possible. "The best way to establish a position of excellence in the NFL," he explained, "is to expect it."

After Kansas City was shut out in a 1992 playoff game against the San Diego Chargers, Schottenheimer decided his lineup needed some veteran leadership. The Chiefs made two bold moves, trading for San

Francisco 49ers quarterback Joe Montana and signing running back Marcus Allen away from the Raiders. While both stars were on the downside of their legendary careers, they were revitalized with the fresh start and led the Chiefs to the AFC West title in 1993. Allen scored a league-high 12 rushing touchdowns to go along with 3 receiving touchdowns and 1,002 total yards.

Montana, meanwhile, added an Arrowhead chapter to his history of clutch performances in a 1993 playoff game against the Steelers. After finding little offensive success in the first three quarters, Montana led two fourth-quarter scoring drives. The first, an efficient 9-play, 80-yard drive, resulted in a 2-yard Allen touchdown run to tie the game 17–17. After Kansas City fell behind again, Montana threw a fourth-down touchdown to receiver Tim Barnett with less than two minutes left in the

JOE MONTANA STAYED AS COOL OF A LEADER AS EVER, EVEN AS HIS SKILLS DECLINED

Setting Records with Style

Instrumental in the excitement and success of the Chiefs' 2003 season was return specialist Dante Hall, who, early in the year, set an NFL record by returning a kickoff or punt for a touchdown in four consecutive games. He saved his best for last. In Week 5, the Chiefs were hosting the division rival Denver Broncos—each team boasting a 4–0 record. The Chiefs were trailing 17–23 in the fourth quarter when Denver booted a soaring punt toward the Chiefs' end zone. Instead of settling for a touchback, Hall caught the punt but appeared doomed as the Denver coverage bore down on him. Hall darted side to side to elude the first three tacklers, and, with the next wave of Broncos approaching, angled backwards, coming dangerously close to being tackled for a safety but instead dodging another three defenders. With miffed Broncos sprawled on the ground, Hall finally turned upfield and sprinted the length of the field for a touchdown. The 93-yard punt return was the longest in team history and gave the Chiefs a thrilling 24–23 victory. "He's a human highlight reel," said defensive end Eric Hicks. "He's like [Chicago Bulls superstar] Michael Jordan. It's ridiculous."

"He's a human highlight reel."

ERIC HICKS ON DANTE HALL

game. Then, after missing an earlier field goal that would have won the game, Chiefs kicker Nick Lowery went from scapegoat to hero by booting the game-winner through the uprights in overtime.

The Chiefs beat the Houston Oilers a week later, but their luck ran out in Buffalo in their first-ever AFC Championship Game. In the second quarter, Montana threw an end-zone strike to do-it-all running back Kimble Anders, but the ball popped out of Anders's hands and into those of Bills safety Henry Jones. In the third quarter, the vicious Buffalo defense knocked Montana out of the game with a concussion, and the Bills pulled away to win 30–13.

The Chiefs earned a playoff matchup against Miami in 1994 in what was a classic showcase for two of the game's best quarterbacks—Montana and Dan Marino. Each field general led his team to points on each first possession, and the game was tied 17–17 by halftime. Marino came out hot and broke the tie in the third quarter. Unfortunately, Kansas City's next pair of opportunities both ended in turnovers as the Dolphins won 27–17. Montana's career ended with this final loss.

Undaunted, the Chiefs reloaded in 1995 and compiled an NFL-best 13–3 record behind journeyman quarterback Steve Bono. In a home playoff game against a scrappy Indianapolis Colts team, Bono connected with wide receiver Lake Dawson for a long touchdown in the first quarter. But Kansas City's scoring ended there, as kicker Lin Elliott missed three field goals and the offense turned the ball over four times in a heartbreaking 10–7 loss. The playoffs were proving to be a difficult and frustrating obstacle for Coach Schottenheimer.

After having made the playoffs every year from 1990 to 1995, the Chiefs did so once more in 1997 with the help of such players as rookie tight end Tony Gonzalez, quarterback Elvis Grbac, and guard Will Shields. But after losing 14–10 to the Denver Broncos in the postseason, the Chiefs slipped from atop the AFC West. After his team dropped to 7–9 in 1998, Schottenheimer resigned.

FAST AND RELENTLESS LINEBACKER DERRICK THOMAS FORCED 41 TOTAL FUMBLES

THE CHIEFS-RAIDERS RIVALRY REMAINED A HEATED ONE IN THE 2000s

Arrowhead Ups and Downs

unther Cunningham, who'd been the Chiefs' defensive coordinator, took over as head coach for the next two seasons—going 9–7 in 1999 and 7–9 in 2000 before being fired. His termination may not have been so much about poor performance as it was about Kansas City's eagerness to snatch up coach Dick Vermeil, who in 1999 had led the high-scoring St. Louis Rams to a Super Bowl victory.

Kansas City further overhauled its team by filling two key positions with former Rams quarterback Trent Green and Baltimore Ravens running back Priest Holmes. The new pieces really started to click in 2002, and Holmes ran wild behind tackle Willie Roaf and guard Brian Waters, the dominant left side on one of the league's best offensive lines. Not just a rusher, Holmes led the team with 70 receptions and tallied an AFC-best 2,287 total yards and 24 touchdowns. "He is doing stuff that has never been done in the

PRIEST HOLMES WAS KNOWN FOR HIS HIGH-STEPPING STYLE AND GOAL-LINE LEAPS

Derrick Thomas

LINEBACKER / CHIEFS SEASONS: 1989–99 / HEIGHT: 6-FOOT-3 / WEIGHT: 243 POUNDS

Derrick Thomas's contributions to the Chiefs were almost beyond measure. More than any other player, he changed the face and fortunes of the franchise when the Chiefs most needed it. "Derrick was the living embodiment of that Arrowhead Stadium noise," *Sports Illustrated* writer Michael Silver said. "It just seemed like he got his pass rush started a second earlier than the ball was snapped." Known for his "sack and strip" move, which caused many a fumble, "DT" was a devastating pass rusher who earned Defensive Rookie of the Year honors in 1989. But it was all a prelude to his sensational sophomore season, when he set a team record with 20 sacks, including an NFL-record 7 sacks in 1 game versus the Seattle Seahawks. In the 11 years that Thomas anchored the defense, the Chiefs finished first or second in the AFC West 10 times, made 7 playoff appearances, and won 3 division titles. Tragically, Thomas's career was cut short in 1999 when he died after a heart attack as a result of injuries suffered in a car accident. On January 31, 2009, Thomas was elected to the Pro Football Hall of Fame.

history of the NFL, especially with those touchdowns," Gonzalez said of the electrifying halfback.

Dangerous kick returner Dante Hall also broke out that year with two punts and a kickoff returned for touchdowns. Just 5-foot-8 and with a low center of gravity, Hall had an uncanny ability to start, stop, and change directions faster than anyone else on the field, earning him such nicknames as "The Human Joystick" and "X-Man."

Despite all the individual successes, the Chiefs ended the season 8–8. But in 2003, the offense was even better, scoring a club-record 484 points as Holmes rolled up an NFL-record 27 touchdowns. Meanwhile, a balanced defense led the league in turnover ratio. Hall also improved, scoring touchdowns on two punts and two kickoff returns. The high-powered Chiefs went 13–3 to easily win the AFC West.

LARRY JOHNSON HAD TWO HUGE KANSAS CITY SEASONS (2005 AND 2006)

At home in Arrowhead for the playoffs, the Chiefs hosted the Colts in what turned out to be an offensive shootout. Holmes gouged the Indianapolis defense for 176 rushing yards and 2 touchdowns. But in a game in which there was little margin for error, he also fumbled away the game's only turnover, and the Chiefs were outgunned 38–31.

he following season, a struggling defense dropped Kansas City to a disappointing 7–9 record, and Holmes suffered an injury that marked the beginning of the end of his career. On the bright side, his backup, Larry Johnson, was impressive as he bulldozed through defenders. On the other side of the ball, rookie defensive end Jared Allen emerged as a relentless pass rusher.

The Chiefs improved to 10–6 in 2005 but narrowly missed the playoffs, and Vermeil retired. In 2006, new coach Herm Edwards focused his offense on Johnson, handing him the ball for an NFL-record 416 rushing attempts, and the workhorse back helped carry the Chiefs back into the postseason. But in another first-round meeting with Indianapolis, the Chiefs were overwhelmed in a 23–8 loss.

Kansas City plummeted to 4–12 in 2007, finishing the year with nine straight losses. "We're underachievers," said Gonzalez after the season. "It's embarrassing. It's frustrating. I think it's ridiculous. We're one of the worst teams in the NFL, record-wise. That's something I never thought would happen out here in Kansas City."

Plowing the Road

From 2001 through 2010, the Chiefs seemed unusually blessed in the running backs department. Beginning with Priest Holmes, who was replaced by Larry Johnson, and finally Jamaal Charles, the three halfbacks combined to earn six Pro Bowl selections. But the runners themselves were only part of the story. Over the course of that decade, a trio of Kansas City offensive linemen—Brian Waters, Will Shields, and Willie Roaf—collectively earned 15 Pro Bowl trips of their own. Also plowing the road during some of those same years were superb tight end Tony Gonzalez and bone-crunching fullback Tony Richardson. Altogether, they helped Holmes set an NFL record for rushing touchdowns in 2003, protected Johnson as he rushed a record-setting 416 times in 2006, and guided Charles to an astounding 6.4 yards per carry in 2010. Although the rushers were the ones who made the highlight reels and record books, the workhorses blazing the trail didn't seem to mind the lack of attention. "I can't really explain it," Richardson said of run blocking. "But it just means more to me helping someone else achieve glory. There's something about it that feels right to me."

WILL SHIELDS NEVER MISSED A GAME IN HIS 14-SEASON CHIEFS CAREER

TONY GONZALEZ SCORED 10 OR MORE TOUCHDOWNS IN A SEASON 3 TIMES

DWAYNE BOWE'S BIG EFFORT IN 2010 MADE HIM A PRO-BOWLER

After the season, the Chiefs began building for the future by trading away Allen for extra picks in the 2008 NFL Draft. However, a turnaround would be slow in coming, and after the Chiefs limped through a 14-loss season in 2008, more drastic changes followed.

cott Pioli was hired as the Chiefs' new general manager, Coach Edwards was fired, quarterback Matt Cassel was acquired through a trade with the New England Patriots, and Gonzalez was traded away to the Atlanta Falcons. The new-look Chiefs lost another 12 games in 2009 but bounced back in 2010. Cassel had a career season with 27 touchdowns, speedy halfback Jamaal Charles rushed for more than 6 yards per carry, wide receiver Dwayne Bowe hauled in 15 touchdown receptions, and defensive end/linebacker Tamba Hali led the AFC with 14.5 sacks. These individual performances contributed to a respectable 10–6 record and a playoff berth. Unfortunately, in the postseason, the Chiefs were immediately squashed by the Ravens, 30–7.

The 2011 campaign got off to a rocky start as Kansas City dropped its first three games and lost Charles to a season-ending knee injury in Week 2. But the Chiefs then appeared to right the ship, rattling off four consecutive victories, including a 28–0 blowout on the road over their top divisional rivals, the Raiders. But after Cassel was sidelined by injury, the Chiefs skidded to a 7–9 finish. Still, Kansas City—as well as many national experts—remained optimistic that a healthy Charles and Cassel, along with Bowe, would soon revive the Chiefs' once-potent offense.

Such a revival was not to be. In Week 3 of the 2012 season, Chiefs kicker Ryan Succop drilled a

Tony Gonzalez

TIGHT END / CHIEFS SEASONS: 1997–2008 / HEIGHT: 6-FOOT-5 / WEIGHT: 251 POUNDS

Calling an active NFL player a "future Hall-of-Famer" is often considered either a jinx or undeserved credit. But it is hardly a stretch when that player has accumulated more catches, yards, and touchdowns than any other tight end in pro football history. Yet statistics weren't everything to Tony Gonzalez, who—while playing for the Chiefs—said, "I want to be a complete football player for this team." Gonzalez became an excellent blocker, and it made him one of the most well-rounded tight ends in the game. While most of the game's best tight ends excel at racking up receiving statistics, few are considered great blockers. During one 2004 game in which the Chiefs ran for 8 touchdowns, Gonzalez caught only 2 passes for 19 yards. But the commanding rushing performance was due, in large part, to Gonzalez's blocking, and because of that, his teammates and coaches considered it one of his best games ever. "I think he just got tired of people making fun of his blocking [early in his career]," Chiefs guard Brian Waters said. "Because, man, he was just crushing people. He just fights and fights."

KANSAS CITY HOPED THAT MATT CASSEL WOULD BE THE NEXT GREAT CHIEFS LEADER

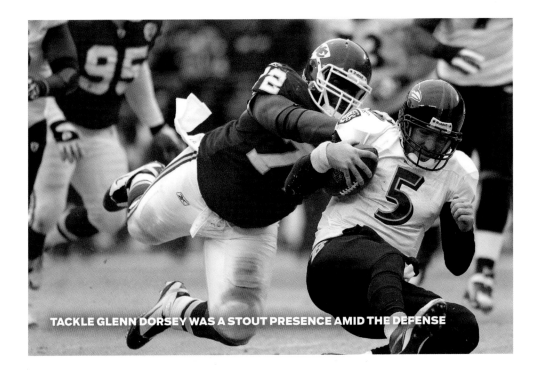

TACKLE GLENN DORSEY WAS A STOUT PRESENCE AMID THE DEFENSE

31-yard field goal for a 27–24 win in overtime—the only victory in Kansas City's first 11 games. As fans were wondering if things could get any worse, they did. The day before the Chiefs hosted the Carolina Panthers in December, linebacker Jovan Belcher shot his girlfriend at their home, then drove to the team's practice facility. With general manager Scott Pioli and coach Romeo Crennel looking on, Belcher turned the gun on himself. Somehow, the Chiefs pulled themselves together the next day and played their best game of the season, defeating the Panthers 27–21. "As far as playing the game, I thought that was the best for us to do, because that's what we do," said Coach Crennel after the game as he wiped away tears. "We're football players and football coaches and that's what we do, we play on Sunday."

The team couldn't maintain the brief surge in momentum, dropping its final four games by a combined score of 103–23. Crennel was then replaced by former Philadelphia Eagles coach Andy Reid. "Andy has always been able to get the most out of guys that don't have extreme talent," said onetime quarterback-turned-analyst Trent Dilfer. With Kansas City having one of the youngest rosters in the NFL, fans had high hopes that Reid's football savvy would be just the boost the Chiefs needed.

From its beginnings as Lamar Hunt's "Plan B," the Chiefs franchise has played a major role in shaping the modern NFL. Its history includes an appearance in the first Super Bowl and an upset victory in Super Bowl IV—a victory that confirmed the AFL was legitimate and contributed to the NFL/AFL merger. Kansas City's cast of characters over the years has included a coach who changed how football was played and players who revolutionized their positions. Heading into their sixth decade, the Kansas City Chiefs are today intent on adding more records and titles to their storied history.

INDEX